NEW YO[R]

PAVILION

First published in Great Britain in 1990 by
PAVILION BOOKS LIMITED
196 Shaftesbury Avenue, London WC2H 8JL

ISBN 1 85145 415 2

Printed and bound in Singapore by Imago Publishing Limited

10   9   8   7   6   5   4   3   2   1

FOREWORD

To anyone contemplating modern Manhattan it is practically inconceivable that it occupies the exact site of the Dutch colony seized by the British less than 350 years ago, or that the modernist Georgia O'Keeffe's smoky industrial townscape by the East River postdates by little more than a century the virginal Brooklyn of clapboard houses and Breughelesque livestock painted by Francis Guy. So fast is the cycle of change in the Big Apple, and so complete, that not a single building remains from the seventeenth century, and few from the eighteenth and nineteenth, while even many of the comparatively recent landmarks depicted in this collection, such as the second Madison Square Garden building, have long since disappeared.

This urgent process gives New York a vibrancy that is well captured in many of these images, from the grandeur of Moran's *Unveiling of the Statue of Liberty* and the glamour of Yvonne Jacquette's view of Brooklyn Bridge to familiar features such as the 'El' – the city's old elevated railway system. But it is above all the upward surge of the skyscraper, here thrillingly juxtaposed with the Gothic in the lyrical canvases of Hartman and Nevinson, and given stylized treatment in Max Weber's futurist phantasmagoria, which epitomizes the city's contagious spirit of energy, endeavour and constant renewal, affectionately sent up by O. Henry in his testy remark: 'It'll be a great place if they ever finish it.'

E D W A R D B R U C E (1879-1943)
Power
THE PHILLIPS COLLECTION, WASHINGTON, D.C.

PUBLISHED BY PAVILION BOOKS LIMITED

P U B L I S H E D   B Y   P A V I L I O N   B O O K S   L I M I T E D

WILLIAM J. GLACKENS (1870-1938)
Washington Square
NEW BRITAIN MUSEUM OF AMERICAN ART, CONNECTICUT/
CHARLES F. SMITH FUND

PUBLISHED BY PAVILION BOOKS LIMITED

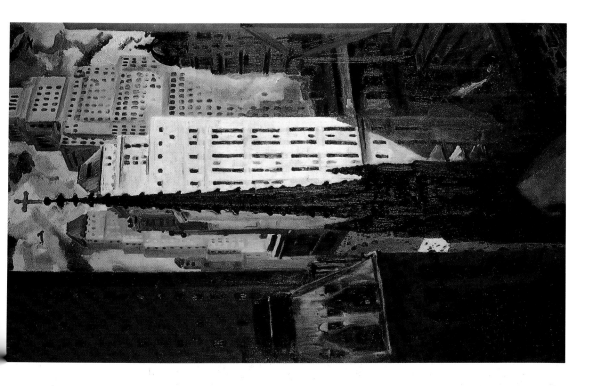

BERTRAM HARTMAN (1882-1960)
Trinity Church and Wall Street
THE BROOKLYN MUSEUM/JOHN B. WOODWARD MEMORIAL FUND

PUBLISHED BY PAVILION BOOKS LIMITED

FRANCIS GUY (1760-1820)
Winter Scene in Brooklyn
THE BROOKLYN MUSEUM/GIFT OF THE BROOKLYN INSTITUTE
OF ARTS AND SCIENCES

PUBLISHED BY PAVILION BOOKS LIMITED

GEORGIA O'KEEFFE (1887-1986)
Brooklyn Bridge
THE BROOKLYN MUSEUM/BEQUEST OF MARY CHILDS DRAPER/
PHOTOGRAPHY: PHILIP POCOCK

PUBLISHED BY PAVILION BOOKS LIMITED

STEFAN HIRSCH (1899-1964)
New York, Lower Manhattan
THE PHILLIPS COLLECTION, WASHINGTON, D.C.

PUBLISHED BY PAVILION BOOKS LIMITED

WILLIAM LEROY METCALF (1858-1925)
Early Spring Afternoon – Central Park
THE BROOKLYN MUSEUM/FRANK L. BABBOTT FUND/
PHOTOGRAPHY: PHILIP POCOCK

PUBLISHED BY PAVILION BOOKS LIMITED

GEORGE BENJAMIN LUKS (1867-1933)
Hester Street
THE BROOKLYN MUSEUM/DICK S. RAMSAY FUND

PUBLISHED BY PAVILION BOOKS LIMITED

GEORGE BELLOWS (1882-1925)
A Morning Snow – Hudson River
THE BROOKLYN MUSEUM/GIFT OF MRS DANIEL CATLIN/
PHOTOGRAPHY: PHILIP POCOCK

PUBLISHED BY PAVILION BOOKS LIMITED

YVONNE JACQUETTE (b. 1934)
East River View with Brooklyn Bridge
THE BROOKLYN MUSEUM/LANDOWN–BLOOME FOUNDATION AND
DICK S. RAMSAY FUND/PHOTOGRAPHY: PHILIP POCOCK

PUBLISHED BY PAVILION BOOKS LIMITED

G U Y   W I G G I N S (1883-1962)
Washington's Birthday
NEW BRITAIN MUSEUM OF AMERICAN ART, CONNECTICUT/
JOHN BUTLER TALCOTT FUND

P U B L I S H E D   B Y   P A V I L I O N   B O O K S   L I M I T E D

W. LOUIS SONNTAG JNR. (b. 1870)
The Bowery at Night
MUSEUM OF THE CITY OF NEW YORK

PUBLISHED BY PAVILION BOOKS LIMITED

THEODORE ROBINSON (1852–1896)
Union Square
NEW BRITAIN MUSEUM OF AMERICAN ART, CONNECTICUT/
GIFT OF A. W. STANLEY ESTATE

PUBLISHED BY PAVILION BOOKS LIMITED

MAX WEBER (1881-1961)
New York
NIMATALLAH/ART RESOURCE, NEW YORK

PUBLISHED BY PAVILION BOOKS LIMITED

GEORGIA O'KEEFFE (1887-1986)
East River from the 30th Storey of the Shelton Hotel
NEW BRITAIN MUSEUM OF AMERICAN ART, CONNECTICUT/
STEPHEN LAWRENCE FUND

PUBLISHED BY PAVILION BOOKS LIMITED

CHILDE HASSAM (1859-1935)
Late Afternoon, New York: Winter
THE BROOKLYN MUSEUM/DICK S. RAMSAY FUND

PUBLISHED BY PAVILION BOOKS LIMITED

C. PARSONS (1821-1910)
Winter on the Skating Pond in Central Park
NEW YORK HISTORICAL SOCIETY/BRIDGEMAN ART LIBRARY, LONDON

PUBLISHED BY PAVILION BOOKS LIMITED

PAUL CORNOYER (1864-1923)
Washington Square, 1900
MUSEUM OF THE CITY OF NEW YORK

PUBLISHED BY PAVILION BOOKS LIMITED

PUBLISHED BY PAVILION BOOKS LIMITED

CHILDE HASSAM (1859-1935)
Washington Arch, Spring
THE PHILLIPS COLLECTION, WASHINGTON, D.C.

PUBLISHED BY PAVILION BOOKS LIMITED

JAMES H. CAFFERTY (1819–1869) and
CHARLES G. ROSENBERG (no dates known)
Wall Street, Half Past 2 o'Clock, Oct 13, 1857
MUSEUM OF THE CITY OF NEW YORK

PUBLISHED BY PAVILION BOOKS LIMITED

C. C. COOPER 1856-1937
Fifth Avenue in New York
GIRAUDON/ART RESOURCE, NEW YORK

PUBLISHED BY PAVILION BOOKS LIMITED

CHRISTOPHER RICHARD WYNE NEVINSON (1899-1946)
New York
FINE ART PHOTOGRAPHIC LIBRARY, LONDON/
MRS ANNE C. PATTERSON

PUBLISHED BY PAVILION BOOKS LIMITED

ERNEST LAWSON (1873-1939)
Spring Night, Harlem River
THE PHILLIPS COLLECTION, WASHINGTON, D.C.

PUBLISHED BY PAVILION BOOKS LIMITED

W. LOUIS SONNTAG JNR. (b. 1870)
Madison Square Garden
MUSEUM OF THE CITY OF NEW YORK

PUBLISHED BY PAVILION BOOKS LIMITED

W ILLIAM G LACKENS (1870-1938)
Park on the River
THE BROOKLYN MUSEUM/DICK S. RAMSEY FUND

PUBLISHED BY PAVILION BOOKS LIMITED

JOHN SLOAN (1871-1951)
Six o'Clock, Winter
THE PHILLIPS COLLECTION, WASHINGTON, D.C.

PUBLISHED BY PAVILION BOOKS LIMITED

F.P. PALMER DEL.

Entered according to Act of Congress in the year 1853 by T. Latour in the Clerks Office of the District Court of the Southern District of N.Y.

LITH & PUB BY N. CURRIER. 152 NASSAU ST. N.Y.

DIMENSIONS
MAIN BUILDING

EXTREME LENGTH	365 FEET
EXTREME BREADTH	360 FEET
HEIGHT OF DOME TO TOP OF LANTERN	148 FEET
ENTIRE AREA ON GROUND FLOOR	111,000 SQUARE FEET
GALLERIES	62,000 SQUARE FEET

NEW YORK CRYSTAL PALACE.

FOR THE EXHIBITION OF THE INDUSTRY OF ALL NATIONS.

THESE BUILDINGS CONSTRUCTED OF IRON AND GLASS, ARE ERECTED IN RESERVOIR SQUARE IN THE CITY OF NEW YORK. THE GROUND PLAN
IN THE MAIN BUILDING FORMS AN OCTAGON, AND IS SURMOUNTED BY A GREEK CROSS, WITH A DOME OVER THE INTERSECTION.

DIMENSIONS
ADDITIONAL BUILDING

EXTREME LENGTH	450 FEET
SPACE ON SECOND FLOOR	38,670 SQUARE FEET
SPACE ON GALLERY	8,450 SQUARE FEET
WHOLE AREA OF BUILDINGS & SPACE ON	173,000 SQUARE FEET
GALLERIES	111,000 SQUARE FEET

CARSTENSEN & GILDEMEISTER } ARCHITECTS
CHARLES GILDEMEISTER }

PUBLISHED BY PAVILION BOOKS LIMITED

AUGUSTUS VINCENT TACK
New York in Snow
THE PHILLIPS COLLECTION, WASHINGTON, D.C.

PUBLISHED BY PAVILION BOOKS LIMITED